FICTION HOUSE PRESS
PRESENTS

NIFTY

December 1952

This reprint edition is a facsimile of the original pulp magazine. Variations in printing and quality can be attributed to the original magazine which was printed on rough woodpulp paper. No attempt has been made to politically correct any language deemed inappropriate to the modern reader.

ISBN 978-1-64720-587-4

www.FictionHousePress.com
fictionhousepress@gmail.com

JANUARY **1953**

ROLL OUT THE BARREL!

Looks like it's going to be a barrel of fun for Nick when the landing is made. Nick's grandpa says that there's nothing like a hot toddy on a cold day, but Nick has other ideas about the heat situation.

It's catch as catch can with Nick and that's just what he's going to catch — if li'l honey doesn't use those keen ice skates to protect herself. We'll end it with the old fly-boy expression, "Happy landings!" For Nick, that is!

NIFTY—January, 1953—Published bi-monthly by Dearfield Publishing Co. Editorial offices, 205 East 42nd Street, New York 17, N. Y. We can't assume responsibility for unsolicited contributions.

Three Wolves and A Wolfess in A Family

This editorial (that's a seven dollar word, bud!) is a quick way of answering a helluva lot of letters we get from readers asking about the other books we publish.

As you can see above, there are four of them—four wolves in one family! If you like NIFTY, you'll naturally go for PACKY PHUNN in PACK O' FUN, ZIPPY and PIPPY in ZIP, and TOURING TESSIE in WHAM.

You can probably get the others at the same newsstand you got this one—especially if you ask for 'em. Nearly all of the newsdealers we've talked to say that they read 'em regularly to see what the well-undressed gals are wearing, so they'll know the titles.

As we said before, ASK FOR THEM!

But if you can't get 'em, turn over to the last page of this glorious gathering of gorgeous gals and you'll find an ad there that'll make your eyes bug out like those of a country boy looking at a hootchie-kootchie gal at a country fair!

Thank you.
The Editor

"100 proof? Uh, er . . . oh that just means you can have a hundred drinks before it'll have any effect on you!"

"Good boy, swami! You not only tell my future . . . you hurry it up!"

"You'll find I'm not hard to work for. I'll even forgive you for laying down on the job!"

"City Editor? Yeah, boss, I'm going to get you a good story on this sorority meeting. You know I'm good at leg work!"

KINSEY-ING THE CO-EDS

A co-ed is a gal who goes to a college where there are a lot of male students so she can be shown first-hand all the things her mother warned her about. And if her mother had once been a co-ed, sometimes the boys discover that the little gal has been warned about things they haven't even tried yet!

That's the nice thing about co-eds . . . they're so eager for education they'll say "yes" to everything so they won't miss anything. They'll even help you with the questions.

Many co-eds are so lazy they don't even want to exercise discretion. Then some are peppy and full of college spirit. They usually become cheer-leaders. One little cutie we knew came to a game one day so full of college spirits she'd forgot to put on her tights. But she got one hell of a big cheer!

Nowdays co-eds take all kinds of courses. By the third year they've usually taken everything on the campus . . . and in some of the study halls. Some gals even take physics to learn how to split an atom in the laboratory but they drop the course when they find out how much fun it is to split a case of beer on a picnic.

Co-eds aren't all dumb, but lots of 'em think a neckerchief is the head of a sorority. And most girls want to get into a sorority house. For that matter so do most of the college boys.

A sorority girl is easy to recognize. If you stop on a dark lonely road with her she'll always ask, "What are you parking for . . . I hope!"

Co-eds make studying a lot more interesting . . . particularly if it's co-eds you're studying. And it generally is. The best way to study co-eds is through their dormitory windows at night . . . or from under the bleachers at a foot-ball game.

Yep. Co-eds sure have a place on the college campus these days. And the best place is a secluded corner where the grass is lush and the hedge high.

"That is NOT the proper use of a brassie!"

"Thanks for saving me, Nick . . . but stop thinking what you're thinking and get this damned life-saver off me!"

"Nick, you liar! When you invited me to your cabin for the week-end you told me the weather man predicted fair weather! It says **RAIN** here!"

". . . And now that you say you feel more natural in that position, explain this phobia of yours about women's husbands."

"You'll have to take off your coat and pants if you want to come in, Nick. The doctor says I'm allergic to wool."

"You can't run me out of here anymore, chum! I bought the whole damned woods this afternoon!"

"You haven't had one too many, Nick . . . it's just my new dress that matches the wallpaper!"

"Surprise! It's only my tree pruners!"

"They're either loaded or she's payin' off a bet."

CLICKIN' WITH NICK

Nick says that Bulbous Beaulah was made to be a red-cap. She could carry two bags and go through a revolving door without using her hands.

And he's a quick and accurate judge of character. As soon as a blonde crosses her legs he can thighs her up at a glance.

His newest gal friend wears the very latest in gowns—most of them look like they hadn't all arrived yet.

And low cut! She stooped over the other night and Nick said he felt like a spy—watching naval maneuvers!

But he says what she wears is her business—and that it's none of his business but her business is showing.

He says he can read her like a book, and has already done it—from cover to uncover.

But although she is a very popular burlesk queen, Nick says he's going to quit her. He's getting tired of the same old grind.

He says he really does try to do all his girl friends good—but if they're lush young blondes he tries to do them better!

He's a real go-getter in business, but he got fired the other day—for dame-dreaming on the job.

But he isn't a guy to double date with. We tried it the other night. He kept us out till all hours, and when all ours was spent he tried to buy a drink on the cuff and got us thrown out of a bistro.

"I see a dark future for you, and it ain't in the crystal!"

"Well, we girls can relax now 'til the next issue! Be seein' you!"

"I was the model in that picture . . . he caught me!"

"Okay! OKAY!! You can stand on your head . . . so what?"

"Shame on you! THAT'S as far as you got with her the past two hours?"

"M-m-mother taught me to always say, "No", but sometimes I s-s-stutter for a half an hour!"

"Mr. Fleming, at your instructions, I followed your wife up to this hotel, and . . ."

"I know I agreed to your wearing your grandmother's wedding gown, but I didn't expect . . ."

"Remember in 'Cinderella' the prince searched for a girl who fitted a shoe . . .?"

Memoirs of A Meter Reader

I first decided to become a meter-reader when I accidentally stood for twenty minutes outside the window of a suburban house and watched one of those guys hard at work. I spent the rest of the afternoon at the gas company proving my qualifications to a cute little clerk who handled my application, and early next morning I started out with my pencil in hand.

Since then I've read gas meters, electric meters, water meters, and some interesting things on a tattooed woman.

When I go into a house to read a meter I never knock. You run into more interesting situations that way . . . like the time I caught the young bride doing her laundry: she had everything she owned in the machine. It was her first experience with a meter reader and she's been doing laundry every time I've gone back since. I convinced her it was part of the service.

You never know where you're going to find the meter. I once followed a gal all over the house looking for it. I would have found it too, if she hadn't slammed a door in my face. One husband had the meter in his living room where he could watch it because he wanted to know what was going on with the electric company. He shoulda stayed home when his wife helped me read the meter if he really wanted to know.

Those housewives sure have a lot of methods to keep a guy from getting a right reading . . . and I like all of 'em. Especially out in an exclusive section I once worked. Sometimes I'd have to go through two or three maids and the mistress before I was satisfied I was being played fairly with. Then I remember the time a cutie offered to hold my flashlight for me . . . but she didn't switch it on. She got an extra charge on the bill for that, but she never complained.

The only complaint I ever got was from Lily de Legg, the strip-teaser. I walked into her apartment and she raised hell because I didn't knock . . . I had caught her with her clothes on!

"There will be no more of that damn finger painting!!"

"Dad, why does everybody laugh when I tell them the ice man's my father?"

"Yeah, that's true, doctor . . . but think of how that 96 cents worth of chemicals are distributed!"

"See, you're wrong! The best things in life aren't *free!*"

"Marcia, you've got to stop this horsing around!"

"I made the wrong move when I jumped her!"

"And can you imagine!—the damn fool proposed . . . afterwards!"

"Doctor, what's good for insomnia? Er . . . on second thought, the hell with it!!"

KICKING THE GONG AROUND!

Nick says any man worth his salt wants a wife and home to go to, but it gets damned monotonous waiting for her husband to leave town.

$ $ $ $

And he says the worst thing that can happen to a wolf is to have a yen for a little hoseplay, then find out that the gal is as stubborn as a mule.

$ $ $ $

He knows a gal who is as old-fashioned as a player piano. She won't play unless you've got a roll.

$ $ $ $

On the other hand, Ogling Oscar says he knows a lush blond that brings out the gypsy—and the check book—in him!

$ $ $ $

Oscar says that since he's a country boy he doesn't mind wearing long woolens in the winter time, but that Stacked Stella wears a sweater that makes him itch all over!

$ $ $ $

MOVIE ITEM: Betty Grable is watching her figure these days. That makes it just about unanimous!

$ $ $ $

Nick got thrown out of a hotel the other night just because some gal was walking the corridor in pajamas. Trouble was the house detective noticed that they were Nick's pajamas!

$ $ $ $

And when Gorgeous Georgia looked up and saw the handwriting on the wall she suddenly realized she was in the mens' room!

$ $ $ $

Nick went political last summer and tried to run for president with a lush young starlet for his running mate. He'd always heard that politics makes strange bed-fellows.

"Me? Oh, I've got a cold and can't smell a thing!"

"I'm crazy about my work!"

"Edna, dear, couldn't you and your magician friend just stay home and make fudge?"

"I meant to tell you . . . I've been here before!"

"I wonder what SHE does?"

"The way I understand it is—that one is the father and the other one is the husband!"

"Seven-eight-get-up, you lazy bum, that's my wife!"

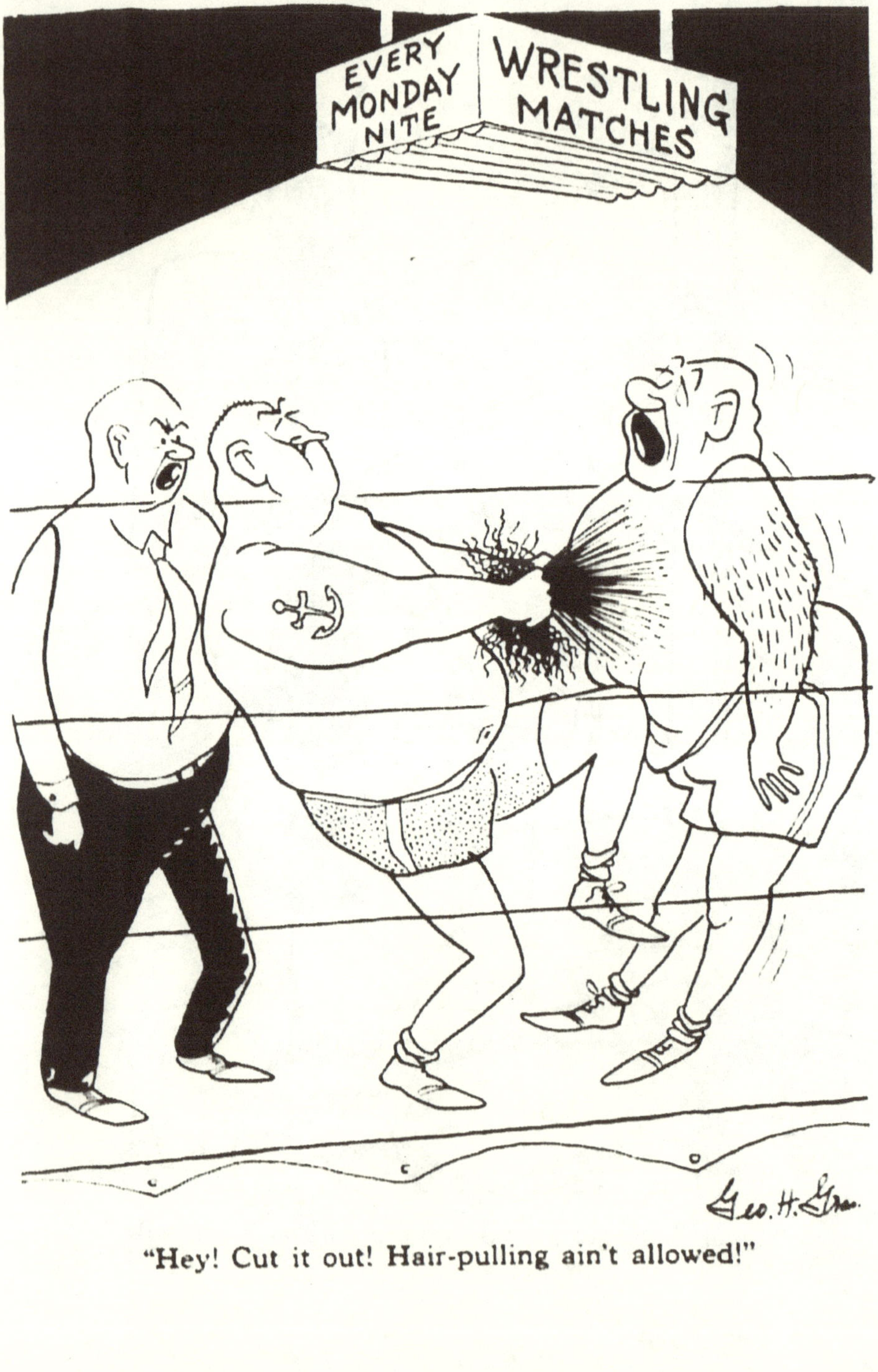

"Hey! Cut it out! Hair-pulling ain't allowed!"

WELCOME
ABOARD

"We'd better concentrate on falsies and a girdle, first."

"Pipe-dreaming again, eh?"

"She says she wants to be a blond, all over."

WRITTEN IN PLAIN WORDS

With Illustrations

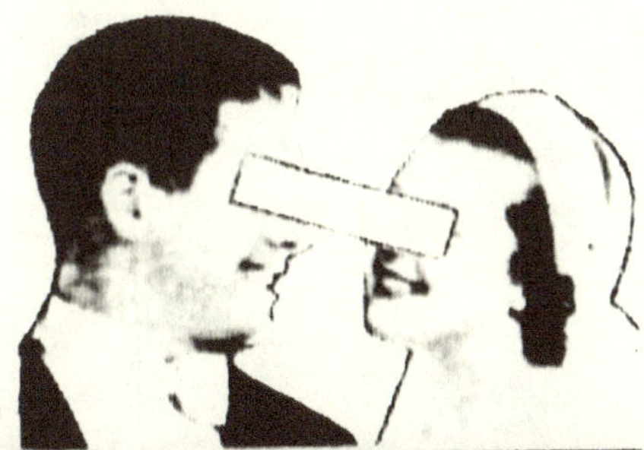

6 THINGS THIS BOOK DID FOR *THIS* COUPLE

1—It enabled the wife to overcome unnatural timidity and shyness.

2—It gave the husband the sex knowledge he lacked.

3—It showed each mate the sex needs of the other—and how to satisfy them.

4—It told how to obtain the greatest joy and lasting satisfaction.

5—It answered worrisome questions with up-to-date facts and latest scientific sex information.

6—It put new life, new romance, new vitality into a marriage that was going stale.

LATEST SEX FACTS

- Preparing for Married Sex Life
- Learn Correct Sex Technique Together.
- Sex Practice in Marriage.
- The Bridal Night. • First Intercourse.
- Male and Female Sex Organs (Illustrated).
- Sex Sensation in Men; in Women.
- Technique of Sex Intercourse.
- Sex Stimulation (Men; Women).
- Frequency of Intercourse.
- Zones of Sex Sensation. • Art of Love.
- Couples With Different Sexual "Speeds."
- Sex Disappointments (Men; Women).
- Sexual Failure.
- Analysis of Sex Intercourse.
- Sex Climax in Men; in Women.
- Secrets of "Timing" the Climax.
- Prolonging the Sex Act.
- Positions for Intercourse (With Recommendations).
- Conjugal Love: Experiments Improve Mating Methods.
- Arousing the Sexually Slow Wife.
- Value of Love-Play.
- Keeping Honeymoon-Love Alive.
- Sex Mistakes. • Sex and Nerves.
- Joys of Perfect Mating Lead to Happier Married Life.
- Sexual Self-Denial.
- Relieving Sex Tension.
- Sex Intercourse During Pregnancy, After Childbirth.
- Menstruation and the Change of Life.
- Intercourse After the Change of Life.
- Birth Control. • When a Baby is Wanted.
- Frigidity in Women. • Sex Starvation.
- Jealousy and Sex Satisfaction.
- Intimate Feminine Hygiene.
- How Age, Sex Instinct, and Health Affect Sex Life.
- Importance of Sex Satisfaction in Marriage.

AMERICAN MEDICAL OPINION

"For young couples striving for ideal sexual adjustment . . . (and) older men and women whose sex life has fallen short of satisfaction."—Hygeia (Published by American Medical Association).

. "Sanely and constructively helpful . . . Can be recommended by physicians with confidence."—Journal of the American Medical Association.

AMAZING OFFER

No matter how long you are married, return coupon for this great book now. Especially valuable for newlyweds. Written in plain words, covers every phase of sex life in marriage. Clearly illustrated with sex anatomy charts drawn by a master. Guaranteed to be BETTER than you expected, or money back if book returned within 5 days.

Make no mistake! Accept no substitutes! This is the book you want!

ILLUSTRATIONS OF MALE AND FEMALE SEX ANATOMY

Female Sex Organs, Front and Side Views . . . Internal Sex Organs . . . External Sex Organs . . . Entrance to Female Genital Parts . . . Male Sex Organs, Front and Side Views . . . Details . . . Accurate and Scientific with FULL Explanations.

SEND NO MONEY

HEALTHCRAFT, INC., Dept. 204-H
247 West 19th St., New York 11, N. Y.

Send me "Sex in Marriage," by Dr. and Mrs. Groves in plain wrapper marked "Personal." I will pay $1.98 and few cents postage on delivery. I MUST BE DELIGHTED or I will return book within 5 days and you will refund purchase price. (I am over 21 years old.)

Name

Address

☐ CHECK HERE if you want to save postage charges. Enclose only $1.98 with this coupon and we will ship prepaid. (Same Money-back Guarantee, of Course.)

"I don't see why you're so angry, dear . . . you heard him say he's just watching his coat!"

"Good gag, eh officer?"

1
2
3
4
THIS ACT WILL
BE CONTINUED
AT
BINSKI'S
BURLESK
ADMISSION
80¢

"Ouch!"

"So! He wasn't too old for you!"

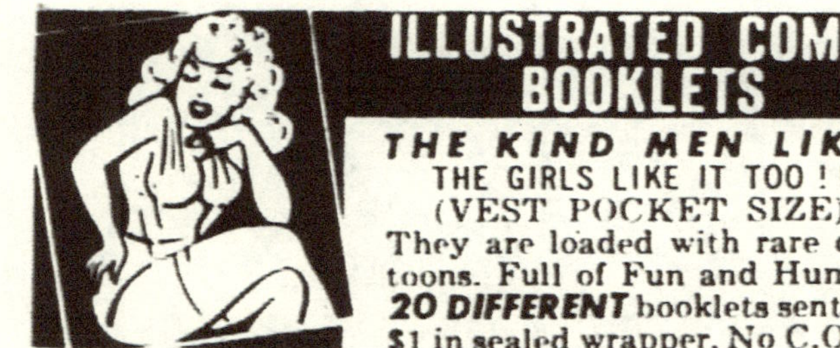

ILLUSTRATED COMIC BOOKLETS

THE KIND MEN LIKE!
THE GIRLS LIKE IT TOO !!
(VEST POCKET SIZE)
They are loaded with rare cartoons. Full of Fun and Humor. ***20 DIFFERENT*** booklets sent for $1 in sealed wrapper. No C.O.D.

BULCO, Dept. 325 Box 382-K., G.P.O., N.Y.C. 1

PIN-UP GIRLS

The kind men like! ... Dream girls. Every shot has loads of appeal. They're thrilling. Send $1 bill for 15 or $2 for 30 different PIN UPS and we'll ship them prepaid in plain wrapper. No C.O.D

BULCO
Dept. AP 40
Box 382, G.P.O., N Y C 1

FACTS ABOUT NUDISM

Many books have been written to justify the nudist movement, but here is a booklet that rips aside the curtain of mystery. It tells you the real truth about nudists, their aims, their hopes and their practices. You will be delighted and amazed at the frank way it discusses nudism from the health, beauty and moral points of view.

Both sent prepaid for a $1.00 bill. No C. O. D.
BULCO, Dept. FAD- 171 Box 382, G.P.O., N. Y. C., N. Y.

Tragedy of the ...
Both books sent ... No C O D
BULCO, Dept. WKT- 174 Box 382, G P O, N. Y. C., N. Y.

FROM DANCE HALL TO WHITE SLAVERY

CONTENTS

TALES OF FRENCH LOVE AND PASSION

CONTENTS

No C. O. D.

Send $1 bill and we'll ship above 2 books prepaid.
BULCO, Dept. WSB- 278 Box 382, G.P.O., N.Y.C. 1

FUN BOOKLETS ILLUSTRATED

THE KIND MEN LIKE
THE GIRLS LIKE IT TOO!!
(VEST POCKET SIZE)
Loaded with rare cartoons. Full of FUN and HUMOR. 10 different booklets (FREE Girlie Fotos with order) All sent for $1 in sealed wrapper. No C.O.D.
BULCO, Dept. 35 BOX 382-T., G.P.O., NEW YORK

"A horrible thought just occurred to me . . . suppose your husband ISN'T in there with another woman!"

"This is interesting work . . . have you ever laid out a body?"

WINE, WOMEN AND WRONG

Good-natured Gertie is indispensable to the local baseball team—they use her for third base.

Nick quit his job as floorwalker in that popular department store. He said it was so crowded he found two women trying on the same girdle.

★ ★ ★

And when Greedy Griselda compained to Nick that he never got anything for her he explained that he couldn't find a man to make him an offer.

★ ★ ★

Nick got to the party first, and the hostess explained that she had bought her very revealing gown for receiving. Nick saw to it that she received.

★ ★ ★

There's a girl around the corner from us who changes her clothing ten times a day. She's only four months old.

★ ★ ★

Ogling Oscar has a country cousin who's still at the innocent age—he knows why a girl's strapless gown is held up, but he still doesn't know how.

★ ★ ★

HOLLYWOOD ITEM: An aged producer is romancing with a pretty starlet. S[illegible] going on 19 and he's going on benzedrine.

★ ★ ★

There are a lot of girls hanging around Broadway who like to stay up with a detective thriller—especially when he's off duty.

"Now, Madame, just imagine you're before a mirror seeing yourself in this gown!"

IF YOU DON'T
SEE IT, ASK
FOR IT
Hollins

Lasting Mutual Satisfaction For All Couples With These Brand New

ILLUSTRATED SEX FACTS

GIANT SIZE BOOK

Packed with

HUNDREDS of PICTURES

Many In Life-Like Color

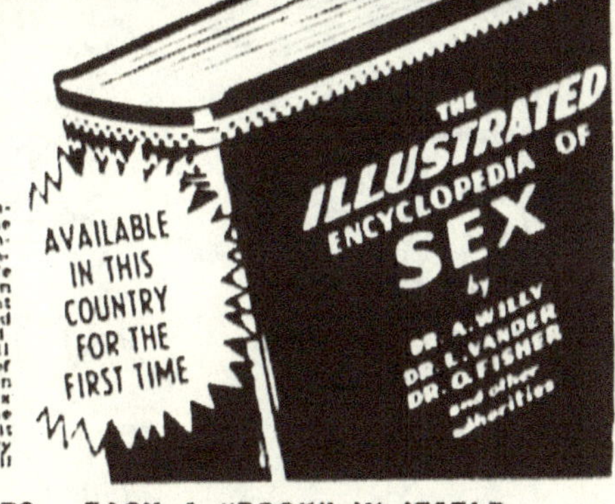

Now available to the public in this country is this sensationally new BIG book! Written and illustrated by the most noted physicians and medical artists on sexual enlightenment. SEE HOW and READ HOW by means of hundreds of unusual realistic pictures (many in true-to-life color), plus detailed step-by-step instructions written frankly and bluntly. This BIG book includes important NEW information and NEW rare illustrations never released here before. Gives YOU the most helpful authentic guidance on sex problems of every kind—both abnormal as well as normal. Clearly see and understand how sex organs of male and female function in action. Many troubled men and women have found a new, thrilling, joyful married sex life and new confidence in themselves by reading "The Illustrated Encyclopedia on Sex." Sells for $5.00—but it is yours for the amazing low friend-winning price of only $2.98. This offer good for a limited time only! Mail coupon NOW!

PARTIAL LIST OF 61 BIG CHAPTERS EACH A "BOOK" IN ITSELF

- Techniques that bring supreme joy to the sex art for male and female
- How woman's climax is brought about
- Female sex hygiene
- Sex Vitamins that improve sexual powers
- Natural birth control
- New discoveries in birth control
- Woman's fertile days
- Showing how sexual desire is aroused in woman
- Female frigidity, its causes and cures
- Causes and cures for sexual impotence in men
- Abnormal sex organs and what can be done
- How to overcome male's early climax
- Blunders made by men in sex act. How to avoid them
- Technique of first sex act or bridal night
- Delaying sex life's finish
- Male change of life and its effect
- Causes and treatment for male and female sterility
- Why woman fails to attain climax
- Male and female reaching climax at same time
- Feminine Masturbation
- Causes of sexual excitement in men
- How male organs function during intercourse
- How female sex organs function during intercourse
- How sexual desire in woman differs from man
- Four movements of woman's perfect complete orgasm
- How sex activity affects weight of male and female
- How to derive perfection in sexual act
- How to use love play towards greater satisfaction in sex act
- Feeling of man and woman during intercourse compared

Just a few of the hundreds of frank, enlightening pictured instructions!

PARTIAL LIST OF ILLUSTRATIONS ALIVE WITH COLOR PICTURES!

- See the Male Sex Organs (inside and out)
- Showing how erection and climax in male occurs
- Pictures of life-like breasts before and after pregnancy
- See where woman's organs have greatest sex excitement
- Watch step-by-step growth of child in pregnancy
- Complete Color Picture Story of Woman's Sex Organs (inside and out)
- Pictorial Story of Woman's "SAFE" days
- Picture Story of Cause of Sterility in women
- Cross Section of the Hymen in various stages
- Cross Section Showing Causes of Woman's sexual ills
- Picture Story of normal Sexuality in male
- Picture Story of Woman's Excitation Curve
- Picture Story of most important causes of impotence
- Two Inserts of Female Bodies showing how pregnancy takes place

...plus many more pictured instructions

SEND NO MONEY!

FREE 10 DAY TRIAL COUPON

Cadillac Publishing Co., Dept. E-274
220 Fifth Ave., New York 1, N. Y.

Send me the "Illustrated Encyclopedia of Sex" in plain wrapper marked "personal." I will pay postman $2.98, plus postage on delivery (sells for $5.00). If not completely delighted within 10 days, I can return book and my money will be refunded. I am over 21.

NAME..

ADDRESS..

CITY.............................. ZONE...... STATE..........

☐ Check here if you wish to save postage, by enclosing with coupon only $2.98. Same Money-Back Guarantee!

CANADIAN ORDERS $3.50 NO C. O. D.

"Would you leave home for her?"

TONY

"And all this time I thought you wore a bustle!"

"How do you like my latest design, Miss Tish . . . oops, sorry if I frightened you!"

"Don't bother me while I'm eating!"

"If Husbands Only Knew—"

If husbands only knew how much they are missing they would not wait another moment to read "Sex Life in Marriage." Many men (even those who have been married a long time) don't get half the delight **because they don't know the knack of sexual intercourse!**

WHO IS TO BLAME?

But this is not all. What of the wife? In all-too-many cases she is cheated out of her sex rights. The sex act becomes a one-sided affair. The husband thinks his wife is at fault. The wife thinks her husband is to blame. The marriage itself is in danger!

TELLS WHAT TO DO AND HOW

Actually, **both** must learn exactly what to do before, during, and after sexual intercourse. In "Sex Life in Marriage," Dr. Oliver M. Butterfield gives detailed directions to both husband and wife.

Using plain words, this famous Marriage Counsellor tells what must be done, **and what must not be done!** The "Secrets" of sex life are clearly revealed, husband and wife fall in love anew—the home is held together! Worry and anxiety disappear. Sex mastery replaces doubt. Married life becomes doubly delightful because the joys of marriage are shared by **both!**

MONEY-BACK GUARANTEE

Mail coupon for 5 days' free reading of "Sex Life in Marriage." If not delighted, return it. You do not risk a penny! Mail coupon now!

SEX CHARTS AND EXPLANATIONS

Female Sex Organs, front and side views. . . . The Internal Sex Organs. . . . The External Sex Organs. . . . Entrance to Female Genital Parts. . . . Male Sex Organs, front and side views. . . . Male Reproductive Cell, front and side views.

MAIL COUPON *NOW!*

HEALTHCRAFT, INC., Dept. 293-H
247 West 19th St., New York, N. Y.

Send me "Sex Life in Marriage," by Dr. O. M. Butterfield, in plain wrapper marked "Personal." I will pay $1.98 and a few cents delivery charge. I MUST BE DELIGHTED or I will return book within 5 days and you will refund purchase price. (I am over 21 years old.)

Name ....

Address ....

☐ CHECK HERE if you wish to enclose only $1.98 with coupon, thus saving delivery charges. (Same money-back guarantee, of course.)

LATEST SEX FACTS

Part of Contents

The Sex Side of Marriage.
Sex Organs Details
Disappointed Wives
Need for Satisfactory Sex Life in Marriage
Sex Rights of Married Couples.
The Female Sex Organs:
Described and Explained
The Male Sex Organs:
Described and Explained
Sensation Providing Areas
When Sex Power Fails
Technique of Sexual Intercourse.
Effect on Wife on Husband.
Sex Intercourse Must be Learned.
When Husband and Wife Cannot Keep Pace
Frequency of Intercourse
The Right to Refuse
Unequal Sex Desire
Pregnancy
When a Child is Wanted
Safest Positions During Pregnancy
Intercourse After the Change of Life
Truth About Birth Control
Sex Relations Before Marriage.
Temporary Loss of Sex Power.
Value of Love-Play.
Driving One's Lover Into the Arms of Another.
Sexual Slowness in Women.
Sexual Stimulation Methods.
Signs of Sex Desire
The Unresponsive Wife.
The Bridal Night.
Positions for Sex Intercourse with Recommendations.
The Several "Steps" of Coitus.
Prolonging Sex Union.
Coitus Without Orgasm.
Easing Sex Tension.
Impotence.
The Frigid Wife.
Making the Honeymoon Last Forever.
The Climax of the Sex Act.
12 Rules for Happy Marriage.

"Best Manual to give." —Ohio State Medical Journal

WITH ILLUSTRATIONS
By Dr. O. M. BUTTERFIELD
RETURN COUPON

"Why, Mr. Landlord, can't you ever think of anything but your old RENT MONEY?"

2 GALS. $5.00
WINE
WINE
WINE
LIQUOR
STORE

". . . And they're not only warm, Miss . . . they're **SAFE!**"

SHORTS AND SHIRT-TALES

Ogling Oscar admits that love is an old story, but he claims you can put some new angles on it if you keep your big mouth shut and talk with your hands.

• •

And he says it's pretty hard for the average middle-aged couple to keep up with the Jones'—especially if the Jones' happen to be newlyweds.

• •

Many an inexperienced girl has found herself locked in a man's arms before she realized he had the key to the situation.

• •

Sinful Sue has turned over a new leaf. After her date with that sailor the page in her diary wouldn't hold another word.

• •

Nick says that once a king always a king, but that once a knight is a hell of a lot better!

• •

The druggist told Neglected Nellie that a certain tonic would build bigger and stronger babies—so she bought a bottle for her husband.

• •

Hefty Hilda wore a wedding gown with a train in the back, and the train was damned crowded!

• •

And Ogling Oscar says he knows a young married woman who's so poor that she hasn't got a gigolo nor a back door to push him out of!

"Just give me a passing mark, professor – class honors aren't necessary!"

"So you think you got mother-in-law troubles—my father-in-law is a bigamist!"

MARRIAGE MISCHIEF

SINGLE OR MARRIED [illegible] for this [illegible] MARRIAGE MISCHIEF [illegible] Know . . . [illegible] Bewildered Groom . . . The Wedding Daze . . . The Bachelor Dinner . . . Hazards of the First Night . . . Honeymoons, Conventional and Otherwise . . . From Smoker to Bedroom . . . The Truth About Trousseaux . . . And many more [illegible] topics to keep you [illegible]. An ideal [illegible] anniversary gift.
TRY MARRIAGE MISCHIEF 10 DAYS AT OUR EXPENSE. Money back if not satisfied. C.O.D. pay postman 98¢ plus postage. If you send 98¢, we pay postage.

PLAZA BOOK CO., Dept. A-911
109 Broad St., New York 4, N. Y.

WRITE *Thrilling* LOVE LETTERS

No longer need your letters be dry, awkward or uninteresting. HOW TO WRITE LOVE LETTERS is a complete book that shows you how everyday things can sound thrilling. It helps you to express your *personality* in every letter you write. This new book contains dozens of actual sample letters that show you just how to write love letters from beginning to end.

PARTIAL CONTENTS

How to "Break the Ice"
How to Make Everyday Events Sound Interesting
How to Make Your Sweetheart Write More Often
How to Express Your Love
How to Make (or Break) a Date
How to Acknowledge a Gift
How to "Make Up"
How to Say "Those Little Things"
How to Make Him (or Her) Miss You
How to Propose by Letter

PLAZA BOOK CO. Dept. L-941
109 Broad St., New York 4, N. Y.
Send HOW TO WRITE LOVE LETTERS in plain wrapper on Money-Back Offer. If not delighted, I may return in 10 days and price will be refunded.
☐ **I enclose 98c. Send prepaid.**
☐ **Send COD. I'll pay postman 98c plus postage**
Name . . . .
Address . . . .
City . . . . **Zone** . . **State** . . . . .
Canada & Foreign—$1.25 with order

"This is my little brother. He'll get the ball for us, when it rolls under the table."

ONE WAY
LOADING ZONE
JACK VESEI

"I see you made it all right."

HONEYMOON LOVE CAN Last Forever
with these
SEX
FACTS FOR
ADULTS ONLY!
HOW TO ATTAIN AND PRACTICE
THE IDEAL SEX LIFE
By Dr. J. Rutgers
70 INTIMATE, FRANK CHAPTERS FOR ALL AGES
Thousands of readers of th s all complete book (one of the largest on sex) have learned so much more than they thought possible! Practically every type of sex problem and every age is individually treated. Everything that there is to be known about sex and how to carry out the detailed instructions. Will help you experience the supreme joy of a longer, happier married sex life and abolish the dangers of wrong sex notions. The book's 150,000 illuminating words help establish the necessary desired cooperation between husband and wife.
FREE BOOK
PICTURE STORIES OF THE SEX LIFE OF MEN AND WOMEN
LATEST IMPROVEMENTS AND METHODS!
One of the most up-to-date books, the latest improvements, methods, etc., that should be known. This treasure is yours now for only $1.98 (originally $6.00). MARGARET SANGER: "Dr. Rutger's work spreads itself sanely into the lives of people who are not afraid to think." INSTITUTE OF MARITAL RESEARCH, Indianapolis: "the most complete volume of this kind."
SEND NO MONEY!
Don't send a cent. Just mail coupon and pay postman on delivery $1.98 plus postage. You must be completely satisfied that these books will open the door to a new thrilling glorious marriage, or your money will be refunded cheerfully.
PARTIAL LIST OF ENLIGHTENING CONTENTS OF THE "IDEAL SEX LIFE"
READ BOTH BOOKS WITHOUT RISK!
NEW YORK MAIL ORDER HOUSE INC
DEPT. R-576
PARTIAL CONTENTS OF THE FREE PICTURE BOOK
CONTAINING 317 ILLUSTRATIONS
NEW YORK MAIL ORDER HOUSE, INC.

"My wife WON'T be coming for me TONIGHT!"

"Damndest storm I ever got caught in!"

"The boss had me on the carpet—MMMM!"

POMARICO

"Joe, I'm sure you're going to be surprised when you meet my wife!"

BUXOM Beauties

A special offer of ALL-BUXOM art models. If your collection is "going flat", why not round it out with a set of these big, bosomy beauties. 10 naughty poses on 4 x 5 glossy cards for $1 or 25 for $2 postpaid. 8x10's 3 for $1. 6 comic booklets free with $5 order

NOVEL ARTS
Dept. G
P.O. Box 410 Danville, Ill.

A fresh, new line of comic booklets for adults. Rich in lusty humor, with good, clear illustrations. 12 of these little booklets, all different, sent to you prepaid for $1. No COD please.

NOVEL ARTS,
P.O. BOX 410, DANVLLE, ILLINOIS

the Stag PACKAGE

A double offer of stag items to meet male tastes in spicy humor and female beauty. 6 comic booklets,— intimate episodes of shapely cartoon cuties. Plus 10 superbly developed pin-up beauties on 4x5 glossy cards. All for $1 postpaid. No COD please.

The STAG MARKET
P.O. Box 568 Danville, Illinois

SHOOTIN' THE WORKS!

Susie the stripteuse went to the doctor with a sore throat last week, and the doc told her he thought she was suffering from STRIPtococcus.

• • •

Nick says that the scout who discovered John Wayne knew his onions—but that the guy who dug up Jane Russell had put in his life studying a lot more interesting subject.

• • •

Ogling Oscar's always ready to share his apartment with discharged service people—says he's currently trying to speed up rotation for Wacs and Waves.

• • •

And just the other night Wilma the Wave showed up on shipboard at two A.M.—and admitted she'd been naughtical.

• • •

Short-cut Shiela refuses to let even the most attractive man kiss her on the first date. She says to hell with the preliminaries!

• • •

Oscar told his new girl friend that before they started going steady he'd better explain the facts of life to her. Said she: "Okay, and when you get through you can go and explain to Henry Kaiser how to build a kiddie-car!"

• • •

Nick loves the movies. He says he was so thrilled at one last night that he didn't know his right hand from his left—until a strange woman slapped his left one.

• • •

That's all, soaks.

MODEL
HONEYMOON
COTTAGE
ACTUALLY
INHABITED
BY
NEWLYWEDS
PUBLIC
INVITED

"My husband doesn't always take "No" for an answer."

SEX *Is What You Make It!*

ONLY $1.98

from FREUD to KINSEY

Your "sexcess" depends on when, where, now, how much, with whom—and a lot more. It calls for the *right line* and the *sure touch*. And what you don't know can hurt you!

EVERY DETAIL PICTURE-CLEAR

Lay questions, doubts and fears to rest. Get straightened out and "cued up" with the best-selling FROM FREUD TO KINSEY, now in its ninth large printing. All the answers you need in plain man-and-woman talk—every detail picture-clear! Exciting entertainment from cover to cover!

ORDER ON APPROVAL

Order FROM FREUD TO KINSEY in plain wrapper for 10 days FREE examination. If not completely satisfied, return it for immediate refund of purchase price. Don't go another night without it! Act now!

PLAZA BOOK CO., Dept. K-211 109 Broad St., N. Y. 4, N. Y.

PLAZA BOOK CO. DEPT. P-131
109 Broad St., New York 4, N. Y.

THOUSANDS ARE ENJOYING *Rollicking* BEDSIDE FUN

..and You will too when You possess "the Pleasure Primer"

The Ideal Playmate

Here's lusty entertainment for open minds and ticklish spines. Collected, selected from the best there is, this zestful Primer is an eye-opener for the inexperienced, wisdom for designing, merriment for all. Call it a gay evening's entertainment or an ideal bedside companion, you'll dally over its contents time and time again. TRY THE PLEASURE PRIMER 10 DAYS AT OUR EXPENSE. Money back if not satisfied. C.O.D. Pay postman 98c plus postage. If you send 98c, we pay postage.

"Oh, that's my lawyer! He's the darndest camera fiend!"

"If this show comes out of my dividends, I must be re-imbursed — I'm near-sighted!"

"If they insist on using 'that' at right tackle, we refuse to play!"

"I LIKE brown-eyed men with green money!"

FLOUR

YES, meet "her," meet Margot, meet Marroca and all the other passionate creations of Guy de Maupassant. See them in their intimate moments, in their weakness, in their strength. See them all in this unique, unexpurgated and fully illustrated book, MADEMOISELLE FIFI AND OTHER STORIES.

ONLY $1.98

Examine this beautiful deluxe bound volume 10 days in the privacy of your home FREE. Look at all the full-page illustrations, each one a work of art, specially drawn for this edition. If you don't agree that the illustrations alone are worth the price, just return the book and it will cost you nothing.

SEND NO MONEY
EXAMINE 10 DAYS FREE

Entertain yourself at our expense. If you don't find it one of the most amusing yet highly artistic books you've ever seen, send it back, and your money will be promptly refunded.

MAIL COUPON TODAY

BOND BOOKS COMPANY, DEPT. E-6312
113 West 57th St., New York 19, N. Y.

Send MADEMOISELLE FIFI in plain wrapper on 10-day trial. If not pleased, I get my purchase price refunded at once.

☐ Send C O D. I'll pay postman only $1.98 plus postage.
☐ I enclose $1.98. You pay all postage.
In Canada—$2.50

Name

Address

City Zone State

CAPTAIN FUTURE
WIZARD OF SCIENCE
COMET
FICTION AND FACT OF THE PRIZE-RING
FIGHT
THE BLACK UHLAN
HEADQUARTERS DETECTIVE
MURDER TREADMILL
G-MAN JUGGERNAUT
MASKED RIDER WESTERN
BORROWED HOSSES
FIGHTING ACES OF WAR SKIES
WINGS
10 STORY WESTERN MAGAZINE
POWDERSMOKE PUPPET
SATAN SPAWNS A WOOLIE WAR
GUN FEVER HERITAGE
ADVENTURE NOVELS
Thrilling Stories of the Sky Trails
AIR STORIES
THE NIGHT HAWK
GEORGE BRUCE
FIGHTING DAREDEVILS OF TODAY'S WAR
AIR WAR
CAPTAIN DANGER OVER MACASSAR STRAIT
THE ALL-STORY
WARLORD of MARS
ARMY Romances
BASKETBALL STORIES
GAWKY GUARD
BASKET BUSTER
Battle Stories
O'LEARY IN ACTION IN ETHIOPIA
All Star Issue of Favorite War Authors
BLACK BOOK DETECTIVE
BURY ME IN THE SAME GRAVE
GOLDEN FLEECE
HISTORICAL ADVENTURE
ROMAN HOLIDAY by TALBOT MUNDY
HIGH-SEAS ADVENTURES
THE SEA ROGUE
By Morgan Robertson
CAPTAIN HARDY
ADVENTURES OF THE FIRST AMERICANS
INDIAN Stories
BRIDE of the TOMAHAWK PACK
MY LIFE WITH SITTING BULL
The LONE RANGER
April
The Phantom Rider
MAGIC CARPET MAGAZINE
PEARLS FROM MACAO
MARVEL SCIENCE STORIES
THE TIME TRAP
NEW DETECTIVE
DEATH LIVES HERE!
NO BODY BUT YOU
North-West ROMANCES
SATAN'S TIMBER CLAIM
GIRLS of WHITE WATER TRAIL
Oriental STORIES
THE DRAGOMAN'S JEST
PHANTOM DETECTIVE
The Deadly DIAMONDS
ROBERT WALLACE
PLANET Stories
QUEEN OF THE MARTIAN CATACOMBS
LEIGH BRACKETT
POPULAR DETECTIVE
DEATH IN A COTTAGE
MURDER INSURANCE
PRIVATE DETECTIVE
LOVE STORIES OF THE REAL WEST
RANCH ROMANCES
Maid of the Valley
RANGE RIDERS
SIX-GUN VALLEY
Vice Squad DETECTIVE
SECRET of the HOUSE of HORROR
TOP-NOTCH STORIES ... TOP-NOTCH WRITERS
The UNDERWORLD DETECTIVE
FIVE FATAL MINUTES
KILLER'S BAIT
THRILLING WONDER STORIES
THE FEDERALS IN ACTION
G-MEN
GOVERNMENT GUNS
THE BLUE LOTUS
GIVE 'EM HELL
SCIENCE FICTION
PLANET OF THE KNOB HEADS
SPICY-ADVENTURE STORIES
HELL'S RIVER

www.ingramcontent.com/pod-product-compliance
Lightning Source LLC
LaVergne TN
LVHW050936080826
845145LV00004B/1282

* 9 7 8 1 6 4 7 2 0 5 8 7 4 *